# Your Travel Guide to COLONIAL AMERICA

*Your*

*Travel*

*Guide to*

# COLONIAL AMERICA

Nancy Day

**RP** RUNESTONE PRESS • MINNEAPOLIS

AN IMPRINT OF LERNER PUBLISHING GROUP

Designed by: Zachary Marell and Tim Parlin
Edited by: Sara Saetre and Rita Reinecker
Illustrated by: Tim Parlin
Photo Researched by: Nicole Tavitian

Runestone Press
An imprint of Lerner Publishing Group
241 First Avenue North
Minneapolis, Minnesota 55401 U.S.A.

Website address: www.lernerbooks.com

Day, Nancy.
    Your travel guide to colonial America / by Nancy Day.
       p.   cm. — (Passport to history)
    Includes bibliographical references and index.
    Summary: Takes readers on a journey back in time in order to experience life in the American colonies, describing clothing, accommodations, foods, local customs, transportation, a few notable personalities, and more.
    ISBN 0-8225-3079-1 (lib. bdg. : alk. paper)
    1. United States—Social life and customs—to 1750 Juvenile literature. 2. United States Guidebooks Juvenile literature. [1. United States—Social life and customs— to 1750.] I. Title. II. Series: Day, Nancy. Passport to History.
E189.D39   2001
973.2—dc21                                                    99-38137

Manufactured in the United States of America
1  2  3  4  5  6  –  A  –  06  05  04  03  02  01

# Contents

# INTRODUCTION

## GETTING STARTED

Welcome to Passport to History. You will be traveling through time and space to colonial America between 1607 and 1750. You will arrive on the Atlantic seacoast in North America. The colonies (settlements) established here by European nations will eventually become part of the United States. As you plan your trip, this handy guide will help you every step of the way, answering questions such as:

➤ **What will I see?**
➤ **How do I get around?**
➤ **What should I wear?**

Remember, you are going back in time to an unfamiliar culture. Some of the things that you own didn't exist during this period, which didn't have electricity and other modern conveniences. (That's why the pictures in this book are either drawings or photographs made after the invention of photography.) So forget packing your TV, PC, and CDs and concentrate on seeing the beginnings of the United States. If you read this guide, you'll be able to do as the colonists do. And they manage just fine, as you will see.

*The early Pilgrims land on the New England coast.*

## NOTE TO THE TRAVELER

Some of the information in this guide is based on accounts by colonial Americans. Other information comes from historians, archaeologists, and other people who came along much later. These modern history sleuths examine documents, buildings, and other artifacts (things made by humans in the past). Some facts can be accurately established by this

# NATIVE AMERICANS AND EUROPEANS OF THE NEW WORLD IN THE 1600s

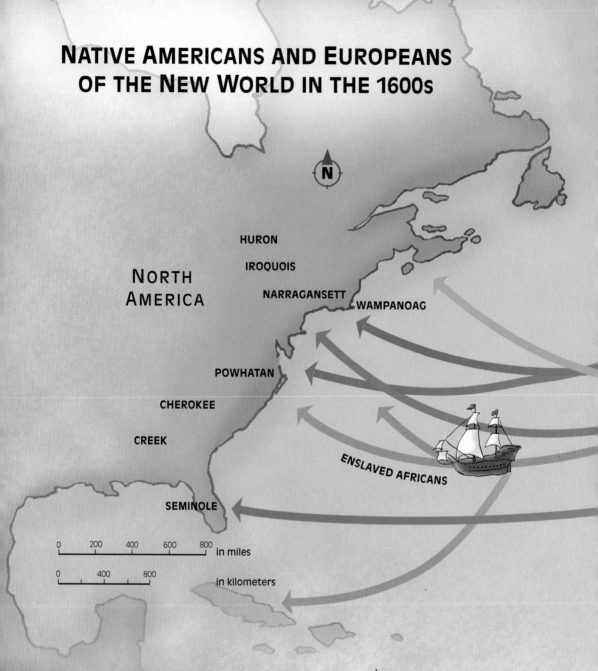

HURON

IROQUOIS

NORTH AMERICA

NARRAGANSETT

WAMPANOAG

POWHATAN

CHEROKEE

CREEK

ENSLAVED AFRICANS

SEMINOLE

0    200    400    600    800    in miles

0    400    800    in kilometers

kind of study. But as you tour colonial America, you may discover some new facts. If so, please report to your local historian or archaeologist when you return.

## WHY VISIT COLONIAL AMERICA?

Imagine leaving home and family, taking little more than you can carry, to move to a world you know almost nothing about. No house, no job—not even a town—await you. Like the settlers, you'll find what colonists

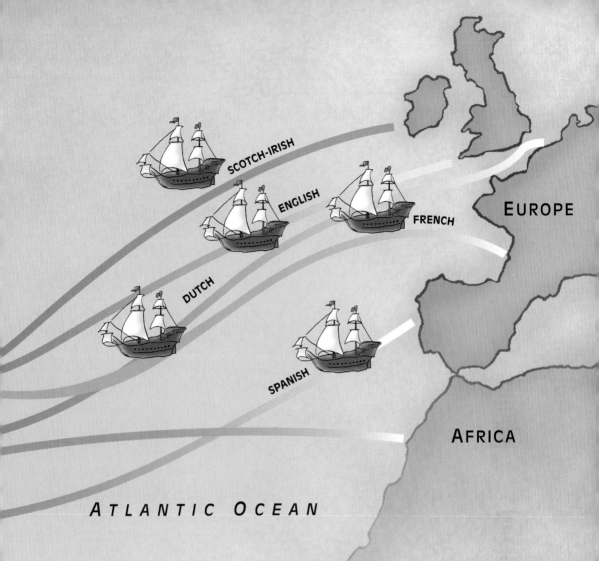

SCOTCH-IRISH

ENGLISH

FRENCH

EUROPE

DUTCH

SPANISH

AFRICA

ATLANTIC OCEAN

call a "New World" where the forest meets the sea. No boardwalks or condos here—not even a French fry stand. Native American people have cleared fields to grow crops. But huge areas of untamed forest remain. You'll face harsh weather, primitive living conditions, and unfamiliar animals. Wolves are plentiful, as are bears and wildcats. Buffalo roam as far east as modern-day Washington, D.C.

To get to the New World, you will board a small ship in Europe and set sail across a seemingly endless ocean. The trip is no picnic. Day after day, week after week, you're crowded into cramped quarters overflowing with people and animals. Your stomach turns inside out with seasickness as you're tossed about by rough ocean waves. You eat insect-ridden food. You're exposed to dangerous, contagious diseases. Sound like fun? The earliest immigrants to America endured all this and more.

African people captured by slave traders and brought in chains to the New World endured far worse.

Slaves were not the only people forced to make this journey. Orphaned children were put on ships to the New World. Convicts in European jails had a choice between being executed or sailing to America. Sometimes bankrupt businesspeople, workers escaping from cruel masters, and wealthy people whose fortunes had run out fled to the American colonies.

Many people truly wanted to journey to the New World, however. Some hoped to get rich by discovering gold. Farmers wanting good land, and women looking for husbands hoped for a better life in America. Other immigrants were searching for religious freedom.

Anyone down on his or her luck or dreaming great dreams could gamble on life in the colonies. When these Europeans climbed aboard a ship, they didn't know what they were going to find. But they were convinced they would discover opportunities and freedoms they didn't have at home.

Of course, Native American peoples already lived in every region of North America. The Iroquois, Huron, Cherokee, and others could be found along the East Coast. The Tlingit lived in the Northwest, the Hopi in the Southwest, and the Comanche on the Great Plains, to name only a very few.

Colonial America is a melting pot where Native American cultures, European traditions, hardships, and individual dreams have mixed. By traveling to colonial times, you can walk among the remarkable people who laid the foundation for a new kind of country. This is a time of deciding just what kind of society is best. The seeds are being planted for what will become, in little more than three hundred years, the world's most powerful nation—the United States of America.

# The Basics

*Chief Powhatan addresses his tribal council.*

## Location Lowdown

If you have a certain picture of colonial America in your mind, forget it. There is no *one* colonial America, and colonists are definitely not in a "united state." Many are English, but colonists come from other European

*Dutch fur traders on Manhattan Island bargain with native people for beaver skins.*

countries as well. Each group has its own traditions and beliefs.

Settled in various places, the colonists' ways of life and governments develop differently over time. The boundaries of the colonies keep changing. Even the names of the colonies change. For this reason, what you find will depend on where and when you travel.

## WHEN TO VISIT

When you think of colonial America, you may think of thirteen colonies fighting for independence from Great Britain in 1776. But Spain began colonizing North America almost three hundred years earlier. French explorers, missionaries, and fur trappers started traveling around the continent not long after that.

The first permanent English settlement in North America was Jamestown, founded in modern-day Virginia in 1607. This is not a good year to visit. Of 104 colonists, 51 die in the first few months from exhaustion, hunger, and disease. A trip to Jamestown will show you how the English had nowhere to go but up. They receive help from Powhatan, a great Native American chief who leads a group of thirty nations (together called the Powhatans). Powhatan's people show the Jamestown settlers how to plant corn and yams to survive.

Native cultures change dramatically after the Spanish, French, English, and other Europeans arrive. Native ways of life are affected by trade with European settlers, for example. Tribes exchange furs and other goods for European brass kettles, iron-edged tools, and guns, which make hunting and other daily tasks easier.

But Europeans also have a devastating effect on native peoples. The Jamestown settlers, for example, eventually begin warring with the Powhatans over control of land. Europeans also bring smallpox and other deadly diseases to the New World. Native Americans have never been exposed to these illnesses, so they have no resistance to them. Millions of native people die from disease alone.

If you visit anytime during the 1600s, you can watch the colonies become established. Avoid visiting in 1613, when English colonists from Virginia sail north to attack several French settlements. The English and the French are fighting over control of North America. In the following years, Jamestown colonist John Rolfe begins shipping a new plant back to England—tobacco. In 1619 a Dutch ship brings the first slaves to Jamestown.

Stop in Plymouth in 1620 to see the *Mayflower* arrive with the Pilgrims. In 1643 four colonies (Plymouth, Massachusetts Bay, Connecticut,

Back TO THE FUTURE

In the New World, you may see passenger pigeons in huge flocks. They will be extinct by 1914.

*Since supplies arrive from Europe by ship, early colonists build their settlements right on the oceanfront, where lumber is plentiful.*

and New Haven) agree to unite under the New England Confederation. Eventually the term "New England" comes to mean the colonies of Massachusetts, Connecticut, New Hampshire, and Rhode Island.

In 1688 in Germantown, Pennsylvania, some Quakers (a religious group) sign a protest against slavery. This antislavery resolution is the first formal protest against slavery in the New World.

You'll find difficult conditions in the colonies until about 1675. Colonists and Native Americans fight many battles. You will continue to run across battles between the British and the French, too. Eventually Great Britain wins control over the colonies.

You'll notice that people who have lived in the colonies for many years still don't think of themselves as "Virginians" or "New Yorkers." They think of themselves as Europeans—Spanish, French, English, Dutch, Swedish, German, or Scotch-Irish. You'll find different languages, money, religious beliefs, and attitudes among them. Traveling through different colonies may seem like going through different countries.

You will see a lot of servants in colonial America. Some are paid workers. But some are indentured servants. Indentured servants promise to work for a set number of years in exchange for their passage to America. Once they have completed working for those years, they can leave their masters.

Like indentured servants, slaves also serve masters. But slaves are

forced to serve for life. Their children become the property of the master. Most slaves are from Africa. Chesapeake planters call these slaves "black gold," seeing them as an endless supply of cheap labor. Slaves often work under harsh conditions. The colonies pass laws over time that give slave owners (who are fearful of the growing numbers of slaves) increasing power over their slaves.

The institution of slavery takes a severe toll on the lives of the Africans brought to the colonies. If they survive the cruel voyage in which they are packed in the hulls of overcrowded ships, they are fully at the mercy of the people who buy them. Families are split up, cultural traditions are destroyed, and religious practices are forbidden.

After 1725 more than half of all colonists can say they were born in America. Colonists begin to identify less with Great Britain.

The thirteen colonies that eventually fight for independence from Great Britain are established by 1732. Life in the colonies begins to change after 1750. Colonists grow more and more frustrated as Great Britain passes a series of laws that seem unfair to them. The American Revolution begins in 1776.

## WHERE TO GO

New England might be the place to start. The land here is not good for farming (the soil is not very fertile, and the growing season is short). The Atlantic coastline offers many fine harbors, however, and trees are abundant. Settlers use the plentiful lumber to build ships, and port towns quickly spring up around the shipbuilding industry.

*Settlers load tobacco onto ships docked along the James River in Virginia.*

Although you may have expected to find colonists growing their own food, making their own tools, and weaving their own fabric, many goods are shipped from England. Colonists also export tobacco, furs, and other goods. The ongoing need for trade abroad means that port towns are central to life in the colonies.

Merchants, artisans, fishers, and many others live in New England port towns. Local families live close enough to walk to the town center, meet once a week at a central market, and attend church together. They often meet people coming in on ships from Europe, so they are up to date on events there.

Many of the people in New England are English Puritans. Puritans were a group within England's official church, the Church of England. They believed the church had become impure and wanted to reform it. Persecuted in England for their beliefs, they came to New England seeking religious freedom. (Some of the people on the *Mayflower* were Puritans, too. But they believed the Church of England could not be reformed. Because they separated from the church instead of trying to reform it, they were called Separatists.)

You'll also want to see the Chesapeake region. The colonies of Virginia and Maryland lie in this area along Chesapeake Bay. Settlers can easily grow tobacco in the fertile soil here. Then they ship it to Europe, where it is sold.

In the Chesapeake region, the colonists are mostly unmarried men. (Before 1680 there are six men for every woman.) Most are Anglican—meaning they belong to the Church of England. Unlike New Englanders, these bachelors desire wealth, not religious freedom. Most plan to return to England when their fortunes are made.

Farmers in the Chesapeake region run large farms called plantations. They rely on servants, slaves, and ex-convicts to do most of the work. Even small plantations use servants to help with fieldwork and household work. Plantations are like small towns. A plantation might have a blacksmith, a shoemaker, and many other kinds of workers.

Plantation life is brutal. The hard work, combined with diseases such as malaria, makes for many early deaths in this region. Half of the children die before they turn twenty.

The colonies of Virginia and Maryland are considered southern colonies. You'll want to visit the other southern colonies, too. They are North Carolina, South Carolina, and Georgia. Many colonists live on

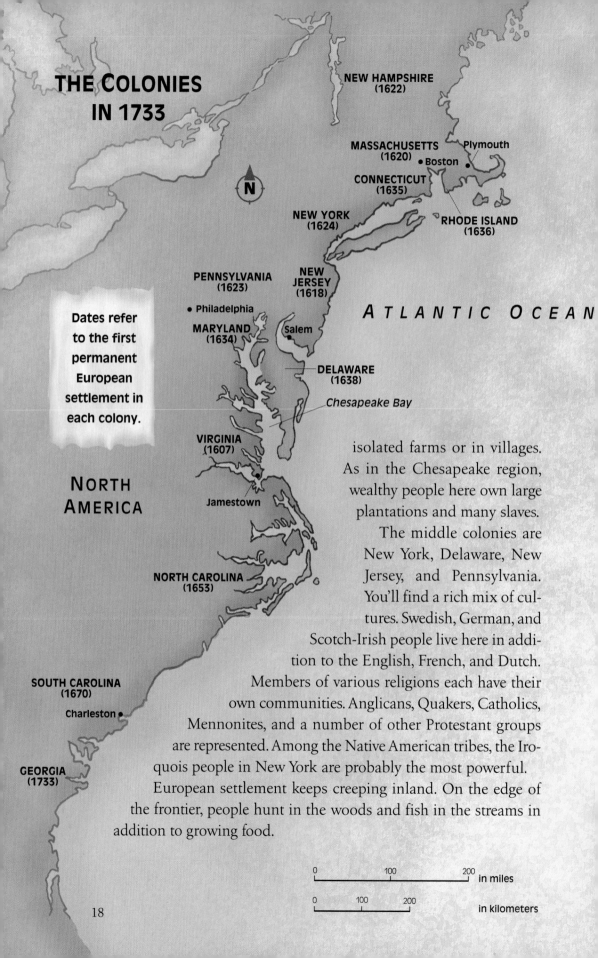

# THE COLONIES IN 1733

**NEW HAMPSHIRE**
**(1622)**

**MASSACHUSETTS** Plymouth
**(1620)** ● Boston ●

**CONNECTICUT**
**(1635)**

**RHODE ISLAND**
**(1636)**

**NEW YORK**
**(1624)**

**PENNSYLVANIA**
**(1623)**

**NEW JERSEY**
**(1618)**

● Philadelphia

**MARYLAND**
**(1634)** Salem ■

**ATLANTIC OCEAN**

Dates refer to the first permanent European settlement in each colony.

**DELAWARE**
**(1638)**

Chesapeake Bay

**VIRGINIA**
**(1607)**

**NORTH AMERICA**

Jamestown

**NORTH CAROLINA**
**(1653)**

**SOUTH CAROLINA**
**(1670)**

Charleston ●

**GEORGIA**
**(1733)**

isolated farms or in villages. As in the Chesapeake region, wealthy people here own large plantations and many slaves.

The middle colonies are New York, Delaware, New Jersey, and Pennsylvania. You'll find a rich mix of cultures. Swedish, German, and Scotch-Irish people live here in addition to the English, French, and Dutch. Members of various religions each have their own communities. Anglicans, Quakers, Catholics, Mennonites, and a number of other Protestant groups are represented. Among the Native American tribes, the Iroquois people in New York are probably the most powerful. European settlement keeps creeping inland. On the edge of the frontier, people hunt in the woods and fish in the streams in addition to growing food.

| 0 | 100 | 200 |
|---|---|---|

in miles

| 0 | 100 | 200 |
|---|---|---|

in kilometers

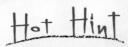

# LOCAL TIME

If you travel in the early colonial years, you'll have trouble finding a watch or clock. In the country, farmers don't really care what time it is. They simply work during daylight hours. When the sun goes down, they quit.

In New England towns, residents are more concerned about time. Along the street in front of the houses, you'll see sundials. Some houses have a mark on a windowsill or on the frame around the front door. As shadows fall on the mark, people know it's noon. Some people use hourglasses. It takes an hour for sand to trickle from the top compartment of an hourglass to the lower compartment.

Since not everyone has an accurate way of learning the time, they have other ways of knowing when important events are starting. You'll know when church services are about to begin, for example, when you hear a loud bell, drum, horn, or gunshot from the church grounds.

You might not even be able to determine what day it is in colonial America, especially if you travel from one colony to another. English

*Colonists use sundials to tell time.*

19

*A drummer announces that a church service is about to begin.*

settlers use the Old Style (Julian) calendar until 1752, while the Dutch, Swedes, and Germans use the New Style (Gregorian) calendar. There's a ten-day difference between the two calendars. For this reason, you won't find a single holiday that is celebrated on the same day throughout colonial America.

You may notice that colonists often discuss the phases of the moon. They time many activities around the movements of the moon as well as the changing positions of the stars. Farmers slaughter cows during the full moon, for example, because they think the meat is juicier then. They wouldn't think of picking apples during the "dark of the moon" (the new moon) because they think the apples will rot.

# LANGUAGE LESSON

You'll hear lots of different lingos in colonial America. People mostly speak the languages of their native countries. Those who speak English speak it with a British accent. They also use words unfamiliar to modern Americans, so you may have difficulty understanding them.

Colonists constantly add words to the English language. If you visit in the mid-1700s, you'll hear newly minted words such as *popcorn, snow-plow, handy, chunky,* and many others. *Raccoon, squash, canoe,* and *skunk* are just a few of the words introduced by Native Americans. The French contribute *bureau, prairie,* and *chowder* to the English language. *Waffle, boss,* and *pit* (as in peach pit) are Dutch words.

## THE NAME GAME

Comfort, Patience, Charity, Silence, Endurance, Love, Increase, and De-liverance. You may recognize only one meaning for these words, but in colonial America, these are also people's names. One family has children named Experience, Preserved, Wait, Thanks, Desire, Unite, and Supply. Most colonial names are chosen for their meaning. For example, Abigail means "father's joy." Hannah is "grace." Zurishaddai means "the Almighty is my rock." Many colonists name children after figures in the Bible.

Slave owners usually choose a new name for the African people they buy as slaves. However, many Africans continue to use their hereditary names in private.

Handy
WORDS & PHRASES

If you want to fit in here, you may want to choose a name that describes one of your character traits. "Impatience" is probably not a good choice, however.

# WHICH CITIES TO VISIT

*The families of Plymouth sign the Mayflower Compact in 1620.*

## PLYMOUTH

Remember the *Mayflower?* The *Mayflower* was headed for Virginia, so its landing in Massachusetts is a bit unexpected. You can meet the passengers (later called the Pilgrims) at their settlement, Plymouth.

Squanto is a member of a Wampanoag band. Along with another Native American, Samoset, he helps Plymouth's first settlers survive by showing them how to plant corn, tap maple trees, and other skills. Squanto and Samoset join the Pilgrims for a "first Thanksgiving" feast, along with other Wampanoag people and Massasoit, their leader.

Plymouth is a small and poor working community. You'll see that the colonists grow their own food, worship in freedom, and get along with one another. The Puritans in Plymouth set an example for Puritans in England, leading them to attempt settlements in the colonies.

One reason Plymouth works so well is that the colony is made up of families who are planning to stay in America rather than return to Europe. An agreement called the Mayflower Compact spells out their commitment to living in an orderly fashion. The colony governs itself until King William III of England makes Plymouth part of an English royal colony in 1691.

# A WAMPANOAG VILLAGE

Before the Europeans arrive, thousands of Wampanoag people live along the coast of what later becomes Massachusetts and Rhode Island. Their houses are round wigwams made of poles covered with sheets of birch bark or elm bark. When European explorers and slave ships arrive in the early 1600s, they bring diseases with them, and many Wampanoag people die. By the time the Pilgrims arrive in 1620, only about five thousand Wampanoags remain.

The Wampanoags move several times each year. In summer you'll find their villages near the coast, where the people fish. You may see men hollowing dugout canoes from huge logs. Women weave and make pottery. Women and children also plant crops.

In winter the people move inland and set up camps in the forest, where they are better protected from wind and weather. They eat mostly dried meat and other dried foods. They line their houses with fine bulrush mats, which are beautiful as well as useful for keeping out cold.

# ST. AUGUSTINE

For a change of pace, you may enjoy visiting St. Augustine. You'll find this Spanish settlement in an area that will one day be Florida. Don't visit St. Augustine in 1668, since that's when Robert Searles, a pirate, murders 25 percent of the population. Visit after 1695 and you can tour the Castillo de San Marcos, an impressive limestone fort that has just been completed. This fort shields the people (and livestock) of St. Augustine during some massive attacks by the English, who are trying to

*St. Augustine, a Spanish settlement in modern-day Florida, was founded in 1595.*

take control of the area away from the Spanish. Throughout colonial times, some slaves, especially slaves from the southern colonies, escape to Spanish Florida. Some arrive in St. Augustine. In 1738 the Spanish governor declares runaway slaves in St. Augustine to be free. This encourages more slaves to run away, and British colonists begin patrolling the border between Georgia and Florida.

# NEW YORK

The island of Manhattan in modern New York was settled by the Dutch in the early 1600s. They called their settlement New Amsterdam. The English took control in 1664 and renamed the island New York.

By the 1700s, New York is a lively city. Many visitors arrive here every year from all over the world. You may hear Hebrew spoken as well as Dutch and English.

Ramble by some of the interesting Dutch houses built when the city was known as New Amsterdam. They are easy to recognize because the roofs are notched like steps. At the top perches a delightful weather vane shaped like a rooster or other animal.

# CHARLESTON

In the mid-1700s, Charleston is one of the largest and wealthiest cities in the colonies. This busy South Carolina port owes its success to cash crops, such as tobacco, that can be shipped to Europe. Most of the residents of Charleston are slaves who grow these crops.

Some slaves pay a fee to their masters, allowing them to grow and sell their own crops. Look for slave women selling African foods such as peppers. They also sell poultry, pies, handicrafts, and other goods.

Charleston is known for its cultural attractions. After 1732 you'll find wonderful concerts here. Visit in 1733 to hear the first song recital in America. By 1735 you can enjoy opera.

*During the 1700s, Charleston, South Carolina, is a large waterfront settlement with a bustling harbor.*

# MONEY MATTERS

*This couple in a typical colonial dry-goods store examines fancy cloth.*

## A PIGLET FOR YOUR THOUGHTS

Money gets confusing in the colonies, so pay attention here. Colonists are still using currency from their homelands. You'll find Dutch guilders, German talers, Spanish coins ("pieces of eight"), and English pounds, shillings, and pence all used as money.

Colonists also barter, which means trading something you own (like a piglet) for something you need (gunpowder, for example). In Virginia people usually barter with tobacco. Before 1639 a tavern dinner costs six pounds of tobacco.

To get the best deals when bartering and paying, you need to know the rules. Let's say you walk into a country store and ask what something costs. The shopkeeper will probably ask, "What do you pay in?" You should say "pay" if you need to barter. But if you have Spanish coins, say "pay as money." You'll get a better deal. English silver coins are worth even more. If you have them, say "hard money."

You can also ask for "trust." That's the "buy now, pay later" plan familiar to modern credit card holders. Unless you know the shopkeeper, however, you may not be able to make purchases on credit.

Another form of bartering is common in New England cities. Let's say you have your grain ground into flour. The person doing the work will likely keep part of the grain as payment. People here often give each other credit for services they've performed. They pay off debts as they perform more services.

The economy in colonial America is generally strong. Watch out for hard times, though. In the early 1730s, for example, Europe is having economic problems, and Europeans aren't buying as many American goods. Some American businesses shut down. Many colonists lose their jobs, and some have to beg in the streets.

# Prices
## OF COMMON GOODS

(1 English pound in Massachusetts in 1680 = approximately $800 in modern currency)

Cost to build 1 average home (1680)—50 pounds

Yearly salary for a minister (1680)—83 pounds

Yearly salary for a common laborer (1680)—36 pounds

Yearly income from a gentleman's estate in Virginia—1,000 pounds

Yearly income from a small farmer's land—10 pounds

# How to Get Around

*One way to travel in colonial America is by coach.*

## By Land

By far the most common way to travel in the colonies is to walk. Ten hours of walking should take you about thirty miles down the road. Walking works especially well in New England, where people live near each other.

Town streets are poorly paved, dirty, and sometimes muddy. So you'll want to protect your clothes and shoes. Women wear a kind of platform clog (sometimes called pattens or goloe-shoes) that keep their feet above the muck. Men wear protectors for their pants called sherry-vallies or spatter-dashes.

In the southern colonies, people spread out and need to travel more often than people in New England. Whether taking a trip to church ten miles away or driving cattle to market fifty miles away, southern colonists are often on the move.

In the early colonial years, roads are just narrow paths through the woods. You'll find them passable if you're riding a horse. Use a pack train (a team of horses) to carry heavy loads. Don't venture off the main paths. Smaller paths may not be passable even on horseback.

By the mid-1700s, the colonies are connected by a network of roads broad enough for coaches and carriages. Some roads wind through fenced farm fields. You may have to get off your horse repeatedly to open and close gates. Don't expect road signs. Local people know where the roads go—strangers are on their own.

Horses are not as easy to get as you might think. They aren't native to America. During the early colonial years, they have to be brought over from Europe. Horses require land, food, saddles, and other expensive equipment. If you do find a horse to buy or hire, expect it to be somewhat smaller than modern horses.

If you can't find a horse, you may be able to buy a ride on a coach. These horse-drawn vehicles carry not only people but also mail from one town to another.

# BY WATER

The earliest settlements in the colonies are all built along the Atlantic coast or on a river. This is because colonists find it easiest to travel and transport goods by water. Cities tend to grow up in places with good harbors. For example, Boston, Philadelphia, New York, Baltimore, and Charleston all have busy ports.

In some areas, you will find ferryboats to carry you across bodies of water. These boats are often just rafts or canoes. If you are traveling on horseback, your horse will have to swim alongside the ferry as it takes you and your belongings across. Don't expect dependable service from a ferry. Ferries run whenever their owners feel like working. The cost varies, depending on whatever their owners feel like charging.

# LOCAL CUSTOMS & MANNERS

## WHAT YOU CAN EXPECT FROM THE COLONISTS

Work is at the heart of colonial America. Everyone pitches in to grow food, build houses and farm buildings, sew clothing, and make household tools. Idleness is considered a sin.

Even small children are expected to work. They stay busy from the moment they wake up (which is at dawn, not noon) until bedtime. Most kids start gathering firewood, shucking corn, and other simple chores at age three.

Older children have more responsibility. Before and after school, boys feed animals, gather vegetables, cut wood, make brooms, and perform other chores. Girls help prepare food, sew, iron, milk cows, weed the garden, and make candles and soap, among other tasks.

Colonial kids have responsibilities that may astonish you. For example, don't be surprised if you see a child as young as eight hunting with a gun without any adult supervision. Adults are too busy running the house and farm to carefully watch over each child.

Children as young as six may become apprentices, or workers in training for a trade. Benjamin Franklin, for example, was apprenticed to a printer so he could learn the printing trade. Apprentices are like servants. They live in the master's home and work long hours in exchange for learning skills. The master has full power over the child, who may be beaten for breaking the master's rules.

*Colonial children are expected to work. This young girl is bringing the cattle home.*

You'll notice that colonists emphasize each person's position in society. For example, seating in church follows a set order. The order is determined by each person's "breeding" (family connections), age, wealth, length of residence, level of education, political influence, and other factors. Terms such as "Mr.," "Esquire," and "Gent." are used with great seriousness (and only by those specifically entitled to them). When college

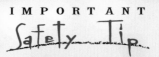
students are listed in their schools' catalogs, their names do not appear in alphabetical order but in an order determined by their social position.

Colonists rarely throw anything away. When they butcher a pig, they use everything "except the squeal." They make spoons out of clamshells and bowls out of gourds. If the hearth needs sweeping, they may grab a turkey wing to use as a brush. They wear every garment until it's falling apart and then make quilts from the scraps.

Don't expect to find a newspaper on your doorstep each morning. The first newspaper in Boston in 1690 is halted by officials concerned about its content. Religious leaders and government officials stop the presses from printing displeasing news (mentions of witchcraft, for example).

If you visit around 1704, you can read the *Boston News-Letter*. It is filled with news from Europe and records of ship arrivals and departures. These are of great interest to colonists, who are waiting for word from "home" and for European goods they've ordered. By the mid-1700s, you will find a number of weekly publications—at least one in each of the leading colonies. Pennsylvania has three newspapers written in German.

# DAY-TO-DAY LIFE

In town you will undoubtedly notice the aroma of rotting garbage. You'll see the flies and rats it attracts, too. To get rid of garbage, people feed it to livestock, throw it about the yard, or toss it into a nearby pit. This pit may contain anything from broken pottery to rotting vegetables to human waste. Hogs run wild through the streets, leaving deposits behind to add to the horse droppings that pile up.

You will also find the noise level hard to take. If you think traffic noise or a barking dog is bad, get ready for the sounds of clanking hammers, squealing animals, clattering carts and wagons, screaming children, and staggering drunks.

This is a tough life. Those who are ill, weak, or lazy have a rough time. Although some charity is available, people in need are often humiliated. In the Brandywine Valley of Pennsylvania, anyone receiving charity must wear a special badge at all times.

If you are used to popping over to the mall to buy a notebook for school the next day, you will find it difficult to get used to life here. The

*A public notice is posted on a tree in New Amsterdam. Watch your step since you will be sharing the streets with pigs.*

*A woman colonist bargains with a trader who has received merchandise from a newly arrived ship.*

nearest market may be many miles away, and most people must walk. The number of products available is extremely small, and having more than one choice of a particular item is virtually unknown. A local may order a coat from London and think nothing of waiting a year to get it. You learn to wait, use something else, or do without.

## LOCAL MANNERS

Manners are taken quite seriously here. Adults give children etiquette books that list rules for proper behavior. Even in the poorest homes, children follow these rules carefully. The higher the social class, the more important proper behavior becomes.

You should know that children are often not allowed to sit at the table to eat. They generally stand at the side. In some families, children stand behind their parents and wait for food to be passed back to them. Sometimes children have a separate children's table where they can stand, going to the adult table to get more food. They are not allowed

## Hot Hint

Children are expected to eat as quickly as possible, without making a sound or looking directly at anyone, and then leave the table.

to ask for anything but must wait until it is offered. When children sit at the same table with adults, the adults sit at one end, and the children and servants sit at the other. The salt shaker is set in the center of the table, so sitting at the children's and servant's end is called sitting "below the salt." Adults and guests sit "above the salt." Be advised that spitting is allowed only in the corner of the room.

Colonists eat with spoons and knives, but they do not use forks until after 1700. Colonists feel that "God would not have given us fingers if He had wished us to use such an instrument [a fork]."

*A Dutch family in New Amsterdam (later New York) at the dinner table*

Colonial communities are tightly knit. Neighbors happily give a hand without expecting repayment. Town residents are treated better than strangers in many other matters, too. For example, a town may not allow shopkeepers to sell things or rent to strangers. Or a shopkeeper might charge a stranger more for something than a resident.

In New England after 1700, con men known as "strollers" travel from town to town, cheating residents out of money. Some pretend to be cultured gentlemen and then swindle money from people. Others fake disabilities or poverty to get charity.

If you show up in a community with no introduction (a letter from a well-known person), the sheriff may give you a "warning out." This means that if you cause trouble in town, town authorities can send you away with no feelings of guilt. You were warned. "Harboring a stranger" can anger people, so anyone who invites you to visit will most likely inform the authorities. That way, they'll know you are an expected, invited guest.

In case a fire starts (which is often, given the use of wood and hay as building materials), everyone is considered a member of the fire department. Run to the scene right away if a fire alarm is sounded.

*The New York Fire Engine Company fights a house fire by continuously filling a tank with water supplied by a bucket brigade. Six or more people use a large foot pump to force water into the fire hose.*

When you get to the fire, step into one of the two lines forming between the building and the nearest well or other source of water. In the "wet lane," the buckets are filled with water and passed, hand to hand, to the fire truck. After the water is sprayed on the fire, the empty buckets are passed back down the "dry lane" to be refilled. Don't get in the way of either lane or you're liable to get a bucket of water angrily dumped on you.

In most colonies, women are expected to run large households. Country women manage a garden, milk cows, churn butter, raise and butcher animals, prepare and preserve food, spin, and sew. In some cases, particularly if times are tough, you will see women laboring in the fields alongside their husbands.

If you decide to try your hand at cooking—and you're female—take care. Long dresses can easily sweep into a fireplace and catch fire. Hitch up your skirts and petticoats and tuck them into your waistband when working around a fire.

Above all, colonial women are expected to bear children. Colonists need children to help run the house and farm, yet high numbers of children die as babies. For these reasons, women spend most of their child-bearing years either pregnant or nursing an infant. You may notice that women's teeth are in worse shape than men's. This is probably because women who bear lots of children lose a lot of calcium, which is necessary for good, strong teeth.

## Now Hear This

The women are pitifully tooth-shaken [toothless]; whether through the coldness of the climate, or by sweetmeats, of which they have a score, I am not able to affirm.
—*John Josselyn*, An Account of Two Voyages to New-England, *1674*

IMPORTANT

*Safety Tip*

In church, if you sit any place other than where you have been assigned, you will be fined.

## LOCAL BELIEFS

In New England, where people live in or near towns, life centers around the church. Religion affects the laws, customs, behaviors, and even the smallest details of everyday life. In many areas, you must be a member of the church in order to vote.

If you travel before 1700, you may have difficulty recognizing churches. Most look like a person's home. The earliest churches have log or mud walls, dirt floors, and thatched roofs. These early churches are often called "meetinghouses." They also serve as a sort of town hall where new laws and other important notices are posted and advertisements are placed. You may find the whipping post (for punishing criminals) nearby as well.

By the 1700s, churches are still quite plain. Inside you will find simple wooden benches. Don't worry if you hear someone mention the "scaffold." Here it means the pulpit, not a platform for a hanging. In the early colonial years, men and women sit on separate sides of the main aisle. Native Americans and African Americans sit apart, in a loft above.

You may find sitting through a church service somewhat challenging. The benches are hard (when you're not standing up), there is no heat, and the building may be damp. The singing is pretty bad, since few people know all the words and there are no hymnals or sheet music. Sermons usually last two or three hours, but five hours is not out of the question.

Watch out for the man walking up and down the aisles during the service. He carries a stick with a hard knob on one end and a fox's tail

*These Pilgrims worship in a simple church. Sermons may last as long as five hours.*

tied to the other. He uses it to tickle the face of anyone who has gone to sleep and to rap the heads of boys who make noise. And no, you can't sneak out early. The doors are closed, and someone keeps an eye on them.

At the end of the service, put a gift (money, goods, or a promise to pay) in a box in front of the pulpit. Then go back to your seat. No one is allowed to leave until the minister and his wife have walked out.

New England colonists use the Bible as their main guide for daily life. Children learn to read just so that they can read the Bible. And they must read it from cover to cover, often several times. They learn fear and respect for God by reading stories in books such as *The Afflicted Parents,* or *The Undutiful Child Punished,* in which children who misbehave die. Adults are also fearful of offending God.

**Don't Miss**

...George Whitefield's preaching during a religious revival in the 1730s. With his dramatic style, he draws tens of thousands of people in Philadelphia.

39

*As punishment, people accused of witchcraft are locked in the pillory.*

The colonists also search for signs of God's power and heed God's warnings. If a comet appears during your visit, for example, colonists may say it is "Heaven's Alarm to the World." Eclipses, the northern lights, and shooting stars might be signs that the world is coming to an end. Colonists believe that failure to promote the word of God—along with disobedience, drunkenness, or other sins—can result in a lightning strike, catastrophic fire, crop failure, or other punishment.

Local superstitions include the belief that a black cat crossing a person's path is a bad sign. So is a broken mirror. You may hear farmers saying the Lord's Prayer backward to prevent rain or see them backing a new pig into the pen to give it good health. Colonists also consider strange behaviors or rituals as signs of witchcraft.

People are sometimes accused of witchcraft in the colonies. You should steer clear of the village of Salem, Massachusetts, in 1692. The village is in an uproar over charges of witchcraft against a number of its citizens. The accused tend to be withdrawn, ugly, strange, or disliked. They also tend to be women without husbands. No one is above suspicion, however. The accused may be tortured into "confessions."

Not all colonies treat witchcraft accusations in the same way, however. In New England, for example, authorities vigorously investigate these accusations. In Virginia, it is a crime to make an accusation of witchcraft without firm proof.

## DEATH & BEYOND

Death is taken for granted here. Many women die in childbirth or from disease. Infants and children die of infections and diseases, and men die from injuries or illnesses. You may witness a funeral, since funerals are public events. Young boys and girls may carry the coffin as pallbearers at funerals for friends who have died.

If you visit after the end of the 1600s, you will find much eating, drinking, and socializing after a funeral. If you can, attend the funeral of a wealthy person. The well-to-do give gifts to all the people who come to the funeral of a family member. Some of the gifts are nothing to sneeze at—scarves, gloves, or even gold rings.

In the warm southern colonies, the dead are hastily buried. In the heat, and with no chemical preservatives, a body's tissues deteriorate quickly, and . . . (well, let's not dwell on that). In some cases, people are buried even before a minister can be found. Don't be shocked if you see people buried in their backyards. It is the custom here to bury the dead in a family garden or orchard.

SIDE TRIP TRIVIA In Europe during the 1500s and 1600s, witch–craft hysteria results in the deaths of thousands of people accused of being witches.

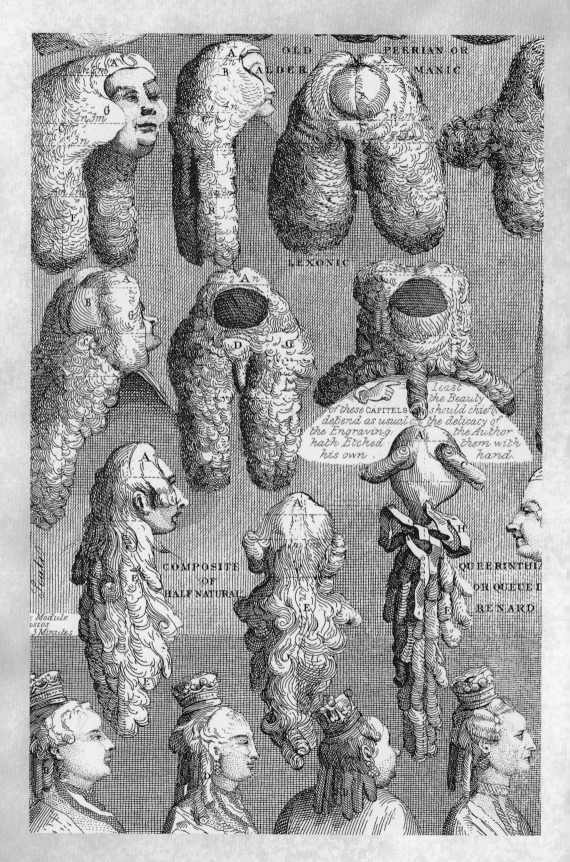

42

# WHAT TO WEAR

## BEAUTY

The first thing you may notice about the colonists' appearance is that most people have many small indentations on their faces. These aren't acne scars; they're pockmarks left by the disease smallpox. Nearly everyone has pockmarks, so the scarring is not considered ugly unless it is extensive.

Another thing you may notice (whether you want to or not) is that personal hygiene is not exactly a high priority. Bathtubs haven't been invented yet. When men or boys talk about "washing," they mean a swim in a lake or stream. Women and girls rarely bathe. People wash clothes once a month, or, in some households, only once every three months (and they don't use deodorant!).

You will not see much jewelry in the colonies. Men wear rings, particularly mourning rings, which are given out to chief mourners at funerals. Some women wear lockets (pendants that open) or bracelets.

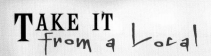

## TAKE IT from a Local

The smallpox came out by the thousands on his face, which soon became one entire blister.

—*a local physician, treating a smallpox victim*

(Facing page) *Wigs are popular in colonial America. They come in many different lengths and styles. Curls of all sizes are definitely in.*

43

*This well-dressed woman holds a fan, a popular accessory. Her escort is wearing a stylish wig.*

Fans are popular for men as well as women. Many are quite beautiful. Fans made of paper and wooden sticks are common, but look for the more ornate double-sided fans made from glazed paper, lace, or silk. You may find fans made from chicken skin, stretched over bone or ivory sticks.

You won't find any tanning salons in colonial America. In fact, wealthy women go to great lengths to avoid the sun. A tan indicates that a person is of the lower class and works outside in the fields. Women wear bonnets, veils, and even cloth masks to protect their faces from the sun. Long gloves protect their arms. One colonial mother reportedly sends her little girl to school with a linen mask covering her face and a sunbonnet on her head.

## Hot Hint

Women wear red lipstick and rouge made from crushed cochineal beetles.

Colonists also wear cosmetics to enhance the whiteness of their skin. Men and women apply flour, white lead, cornstarch, or other whiteners mixed with grease to make them stay on. They use lampblack (soot) to darken eyebrows and lashes.

You may want to wear a popular colonial tattoo called a beauty patch. Beauty patches were originally used to cover smallpox scars and other facial sores. Worn on the face, most beauty patches are round, but you may find some shaped like the suits from a deck of cards or like a fleur-de-lis (a stylized flower).

Native Americans also wear tattoos. Some wear tattoos simply as decoration. Others use them to show where they are from or to signify their loyalty to a particular group.

# CLOTHES

You will need a few clothing essentials for your trip. Male travelers should get a doublet (a tight jacket), a linen shirt, breeches (baggy pants that come to just below the knee), long socks, and moccasins or boots. If you plan to travel on rough trails through the forests, get a leather jacket and leather breeches. Brambles and briers in the underbrush can easily tear less sturdy clothes.

Female travelers should have a long skirt, a bodice (a short, sleeveless blouse or vest), separate sleeves to tie into the armholes, and wings (triangular cloth pieces that cover the shoulders on the outside). Under all this, you'll wear up to five undergarments. The colder the weather, the more undergarments you'll want. Use an apron to protect your clothes while working.

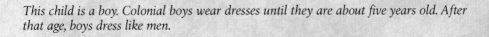

*This child is a boy. Colonial boys wear dresses until they are about five years old. After that age, boys dress like men.*

You will need a sturdy pair of shoes for walking, as that is how most people get around here. The shoes are cut so that each shoe fits either foot. Switch the shoes occasionally to make them last longer. Boots are good for riding on horseback, but they are uncomfortable for walking.

Wealthy people are easy to pick out in colonial America. They wear powdered wigs, hats laced with gold, velvet or satin coats, brightly colored purses, handkerchiefs, gloves, and silk stockings. And that's just the men.

Wealthy women follow the London fashions, wearing richly colored dresses embroidered with silver or gold and layer upon layer of lace. Their shoes are made of thin material and paper soles, advertising the fact that the lady does not have to work.

You may notice that the girls and women here look rather stiff. From an early age, girls' backs are strapped to backboards to ensure straight posture. Their clothing contains stays (rigid pieces of wood or bone), worn around the waist. Stays are also meant to promote good posture.

You may notice that children look like miniature adults. Almost as soon as they can walk, kids are dressed exactly the same as their parents.

*Bright colors are fashionable, and many colonists prefer the color red.*

This means that wealthy boys wear an outfit that includes a fancy coat, hat, handkerchief, and gloves. A girl might wear high-heeled shoes and hoop petticoats

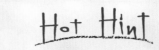

## Hot Hint

Colonists consider it inappropriate for a woman's ankle or elbow to show.

(a sort of harness made with strips of board and steel to poof out her skirts and make her stand straight) under her skirts.

To make clothes, the common folk grow flax, the plant that furnishes the fibers for linen. They pound and comb and bleach flax fibers, from which they spin thread and weave cloth for garments. From start to finish, making a shirt takes about one year. Colonists also raise sheep for wool.

Most clothes are made by women. But men sew as well, particularly during the winter when they have few farm chores. Since fabric takes so long to make and is expensive to buy from overseas, most people have only one or two complete outfits.

Dark red is a common color for clothes in New England. You will also see blues, greens, and even yellows. Don't be misled by the faded clothes you may have seen in modern museums. Bright colors are the rule in colonial America.

You should be aware that some groups disapprove of extravagance. In Massachusetts in1634, it is illegal to buy fabrics that contain gold, silver, silk, or lace. Virginia has restrictions on fancy dress for ordinary people. Connecticut charges higher taxes for people who wear expensive clothing.

# HAIR

Hairstyles vary depending on when you travel and where you go. In the early 1600s, colonists (even the men) wear their hair long. Women wear their hair up and off the face. Letting your hair down is considered overly provocative, although some hanging curls or ringlets are allowed. Women wear hats or bonnets, even indoors.

If you travel after 1675, you will find that wigs are all the rage. Men, women, and even kids wear them. Wigs often feature huge rolls, curls, braids, and tails. The different styles have names such as "grave

## Hot Hint

A wig, like its owner's real hair, is seldom washed. You may see colonists using a special pick to scratch under their wigs—where lice thrive.

fullbottom," "giddy feather-top," and so forth. They may be made from the hair of horses or goats, the tails of cows or calves, or other natural materials. They may also contain silk, thread, or brightly colored ribbons.

Some colonists protest that wigs are vain, hot, itchy, and insect-ridden, but just as in modern times, fashion rules. If you wear a wig, watch out for wig-snatchers. A wig is expensive and can easily be snatched off your head and resold.

# WHAT TO SEE & DO

*The tables in this school consist of half logs.*

## SCHOOL

Education in colonial America varies. Children in the southern colonies are less likely to attend school than children in other areas. Where plantations are spread out, schools are few and widely scattered. Wealthy children are often taught at home by a tutor. Sometimes several families get together and hire a teacher. Slaves and servants do not get an education at all.

In New England, however, most communities have a school. Class meets every day except Sunday. And kids *pay* to go to school. The fees may be paid in beaver skins, corn, beans, fireplace logs, or other valuable items.

Boys study Greek, Latin, science, math, celestial navigation (directing a ship using the positions of the stars), geography, and history. If their parents can afford it, older boys can go to England to study law or medicine.

Relatives or private tutors teach girls. A girl's education focuses on household skills such as spinning, weaving, cooking, manners, and nursing. Girls learn to read just well enough to read their Bibles. They need to write well enough to record household expenses. Upper-class girls may also study art, music, and French.

If you are lucky enough to get a chance to visit a school here, there are a few things you should know. First, you may have to walk three or four miles to get there. The school will probably be a one-room building.

When you enter, take off your hat. Although you probably do this all the time at home, don't forget to bow to the teacher. You'll see that children of all ages are in the same class. Like them, stand up and bow any time an adult enters the room. If the students go from one place to another, they form a single line and walk quietly (don't even think about running).

No maps, blackboards, cafeteria menus, televisions, computers, or decorations are here to distract you. The room is plain, sparse, and dark. It is cold in winter and hot in summer. School is not supposed to be fun. It is supposed to be work.

The youngest kids sit on benches or logs. You will probably sit facing the wall at a simple board desk laid on pegs in the wall. The teacher will be behind you in the middle of the room. Don't expect to use paper. It's

**IMPORTANT**
*Safety Tip*

If you talk in class, you could be in big trouble. Students who make noise get the whispering stick—a gaglike stick put in the mouth and held in place with a strip of cloth.

too valuable to give to *kids*. You'll get a piece of birch bark (or, if you're lucky, a piece of slate) to write on.

Teachers or one of the older boys make pens from goose feathers. Each student brings from home a bottle or animal horn filled with ink they have made at home from ink powder. Dip the pointed, hollow tip of the goose feather into the ink. Try to write in a neat, straight line (no lined paper here). Colonists value good handwriting.

The first colonial schoolbook has only one page. This is paper, cloth, tin, or wood attached to a piece of paddle-shaped wood. A thin sheet of yellowish, see-through animal horn protects the page while allowing students to see the text through it. For this reason, a book like this is called a hornbook. The hornbook includes only the alphabet, simple syllables such as "ac," "ec," "ic," and the Lord's Prayer. Hornbooks are gradually replaced by the *New England Primer*, a schoolbook containing about eighty pages of words, prayers, rhymes, and (after 1750) short stories.

*A hornbook*

Students learn arithmetic, but generally not from a book. And you'd better hope that the class is not studying measurements. Liquids are measured not in cups or quarts, but in anchors, firkins, and butts. Dry materials are measured not in tablespoons or ounces, but in pottles, cooms, and strikes.

Colonial kids learn a lot through rhymes, because rhyming makes things easier to remember. You may recognize "Thirty days hath September, April, June, and November." Other rhymes may be new to you.

Above all, be on your best behavior. Punishments are severe. Teachers beat students with birch rods, whip them with leather straps, or rap them on the head with heavy thimbles. Teachers also embarrass students by pinching their noses in the split end of a tree branch, forcing them to stand on a stool wearing a dunce cap, or making them wear signs such as "Tell-Tale" or "Idle-Boy."

# CHOPPING BEES

Trees are chopped down to build houses and barns and to clear fields for crops. Chopping bees bring neighborhood men together to share in this big job. Usually chopping bees are designed to help a man who has just gotten married, is down on his luck, or is new to the community.

The men start working just after daybreak. But the best part, the "drive," usually comes at the end of the day. In the drive, the men chop about halfway through the trunks of a tight group of trees and then land a few choice chops on a key tree in the group. The key tree falls into another tree, which falls into another, until, like dominos, they all topple.

If you enjoy this sort of group activity, you may also want to observe a house-raising or barn-raising. Other group activities include butchering meat, husking corn, and pulling tree stumps out of the ground. Women gather to make quilts or rugs at quilting bees. Colonists turn these jobs into festive occasions. Mingling gives hard-working colonists a chance to show off their skills, swap gossip, socialize, and relax.

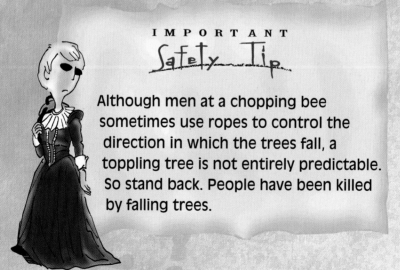

**IMPORTANT**
**Safety Tip**

Although men at a chopping bee sometimes use ropes to control the direction in which the trees fall, a toppling tree is not entirely predictable. So stand back. People have been killed by falling trees.

# HANGINGS

Although public executions are not everyone's cup of tea, they are well-attended events in colonial America. The criminal generally arrives by cart, riding atop a coffin. The crowd gathers around, having brought chicken or other food to munch.

The hanging itself can be gruesome. But you will find this increases its interest for the crowd. The criminal is seated on a horse, and the executioner places a noose around the criminal's neck. (Female criminals are not executed if they are pregnant, but the fatal day is simply postponed until after the child is born.) Someone slaps the horse to make it take off, and the prisoner, snared by the noose, drops down. If the drop is sharp enough, the victim's neck breaks immediately, and the show is over. If the fall is not sharp, the prisoner slowly suffocates. The sight of the criminal "dancing on the rope"—swinging, turning colors, and squirming—is a real crowd-pleaser. Sometimes the sheriff stops the show by pulling on the victim's legs, ending the suffering.

# MUSTER DAYS

The colonies keep militia (citizens' armies) to defend the colony. Often the militia includes every man and boy old enough and healthy enough to fight. The commander of these troops periodically schedules a Muster Day to give them a chance to practice. But disciplined military drill is often only a small part of Muster Day. Usually the soldiers simply march up and down the village green, shoot their muskets a couple of times, and then begin celebrating.

Shooting contests are a popular part of Muster Day. Avoid these if you are squeamish, as the targets are often live turkeys or ducks. You may also find races, wrestling matches, or other competitions. If too much drinking goes on, Muster Day can dissolve into chaos, with fistfights not at all uncommon.

# WHERE TO FIND
# SPORTS & RECREATION

## GAMES

Colonial games tend to be pretty simple. One of the most popular activities is rolling a large wooden hoop. Kids race to see who can get their hoop to the finish line first. If you give it a try, you'll see that this is harder than it looks.

A game you may recognize is bowling. Colonists use nine pins instead of ten, and the pins have to be reset by hand each time they're knocked down. Instead of rolling the ball down a smooth wooden alley, you must use a bumpy, grass-covered hill.

Other pastimes are quoits (which is like horseshoes except the "shoes" are closed rings), hopscotch, marbles, tag, kite-flying, swimming, fishing, or even just taking a walk. If the weather is bad, you may spin tops, read, or embroider indoors. You may see women as well as men playing cards and dice games.

*Favorite pastimes include card games (facing page). Colonial children like to roll hoops (right). They race each other to the finish line. Whoever gets there first wins.*

*Colonists bowl with nine pins instead of ten. Since there are no indoor bowling alleys in colonial America, the game is played outside.*

# SPORTS

A popular sport, particularly in the southern colonies, is horse racing. This sport began among wealthy colonists, who could afford to breed animals for pleasure. You will find horse-racing tracks in Massachusetts, New York, New Jersey, Rhode Island, and Virginia.

Two popular spectator sports are cockfighting and bullbaiting. Cockfighting involves male chickens that have been trained to fight. To make the battle more vicious, colonists tie sharp steel spurs to the chickens' feet. Armed this way, the birds draw blood when they strike each other. You will see people cheering for and betting on their favorite contestants.

Bullbaiting is not much more pleasant. It features enraged bulls fighting off packs of attacking dogs.

## TAKE IT from a Local

There is yet another kind of Sport, which the young People take great Delight in, and that is, the Hunting of wild Horses; which they pursue sometimes with Dogs, and sometimes without.
—*Robert Beverley*, The History and Present State of Virginia, *1705*

# RECREATIONAL ACTIVITIES

Fireplaces are everyday gathering spots for family and friends. A popular pastime is telling tales around the fire. You may enjoy the ghost stories, tall tales, old folktales, or funny stories as much as any modern sitcom.

A popular form of entertainment, particularly for the wealthy, is dancing. Dances (they may be called "assemblies") are often quite formal, with rigid rules. Wait until the highest-ranking couples have danced, one at a time, with all the others watching. Feel free to criticize their moves. That's part of the fun. The floor is then opened up for less formal dances with everyone joining in.

Dances are a way for wealthy people to meet marriage partners. A suitor can judge manners and physical fitness, including the condition of a person's teeth and breath.

*Dancing is an important social skill in the colonies.*

# WHERE TO STAY

## PRIVATE HOMES

If you travel during the early 1600s, you may end up with very simple accommodations. Many early homes are copies of Native American dwellings made from deerskins, tree boughs, and grasses. If you visit in

*A Native American village occupies Manhattan Island when the first colonists arrive.*

1626, for example, all but one of the thirty homes on the island of Manhattan are made of tree bark.

A common style of English house after 1700 has only one room on the ground floor and a narrow ladder leading up to a loft for sleeping. Puritan houses in New England are covered with plain, unpainted

*Virginia settlers build brick houses that resemble those they left behind in Europe.*

clapboard. Dutch, Welsh, German, and Swedish houses are usually built of brick or stone and are small and simple. Few houses have more than eight rooms.

Before 1700 most houses have only one main room, which is called the "hall." This is a living room where people really *live*. They cook, eat, pray, entertain guests, work, argue, and pass their time here. You will find that the hall is dark, noisy, smoky, and busy with activity. Since families often have ten or more members (including lots of children), a house with only one room will seem mighty crowded.

People share sleeping space, and a bedroom is any place where there's room to lie down. Real beds are expensive. You will more likely sleep in a bedroll (sort of like a sleeping bag) on the floor. If you are lucky, you may get a feather mattress. More common is a mattress stuffed with rags, cornhusks, or bits of wool (which may still smell like the sheep they came from).

Even in the southern colonies, which will one day be known for their plantation mansions, houses are small. A typical house is about the size of a modern living room, although it may be set on a large plot of land.

By 1720 wealthy plantation owners build homes with high ceilings, large staircases, a dozen or more rooms, formal gardens, and other luxuries.

The houses will seem dark to you, even during the day. Windows are small and few. Don't be surprised if the windows are simply paper smeared with grease to let in a little light. Glass windows are rare before 1629. Your eyes will adjust, however, to the low light provided by the fireplace.

If you are visiting during the 1600s, don't expect to find lots of candles—they're expensive and time consuming to make. As substitutes for candles, you may find people using large splinters of wood called pine knots, which burn slowly and give good light. Pine knots are smoky, however, so they are burned in a corner of the fireplace rather than out in the room. Plan to rise at dawn and go to bed at dusk to make use of the daylight.

If you travel after 1700, you will find candles easier to come by. Some candles are made from bayberries (you may see children gathering bayberries). These have a delightful scent. Lamps of various designs are filled with grease or oil (which may be whale or fish oil and does not have a delightful scent). Lamps may be hung on the wall or on the back of a chair.

*A colonial woman makes candles by dipping strings into a kettle of hot wax, then hanging them up to harden.*

## Back TO THE FUTURE

In recent years, you may have seen paints in colors designed to resemble those used in colonial times (such as "Williamsburg Blue"). These soft shades of red, blue, green, and gold were mistakenly based on faded paint samples. In colonial America, the colors are bright and lively.

One thing you'll notice sooner or later (probably sooner) is the absence of indoor bathrooms. You'll have to go outside, regardless of the weather, to an outdoor "necessary." Take a few cornhusks with you for toilet paper. After about 1700, you may find a convenience called a chamber pot. This container is kept under the bed to be used at night. It is emptied later, either into the necessary or simply out the window.

Some families order furniture from England, but most buy furniture made in the colonies, or they make their own. Houses don't have closets. Hang your clothes on the pegs on the walls.

Heat comes from fireplaces. Your host will keep the fire going all night. If it goes out, a boy may be sent to a neighbor's house to fetch some live coals from which a fire can be started. Otherwise, someone

*Oak chests such as this one are made in the 1600s.*

*Travelers are sometimes invited to stay in private homes such as this one.*

will start a fire by striking a piece of flint (a type of stone) with a steel to make a spark.

Too much soot in a chimney can cause a dangerous fire, so colonists keep the chimney clean by sweeping it with a broom. If you hear a lot of squawking and then see a very dirty and angry chicken running around, it is because some folks clean the chimney by dropping a live chicken down it. The bird's flapping wings sweep out the soot.

Colonial Americans, especially in the southern colonies, are hospitable. They gladly put up strangers in their own homes. In Virginia, for example, all you need do is ask where a "Gentleman" or a "good House-keeper" lives. Plantation owners enjoy opportunities to socialize with people like themselves. They live far from cities and don't often have a chance to meet new people. Even poor families with only one bed will make room for a tired traveler.

# Public Accommodations

Most cities in New England have an inn. (Ask for the "ordinary," or tavern.) Here you will find not only food and shelter but also good conversation. Among the common topics are politics, news, religion, business, and even history and science. Your fellow travelers from different areas and with varying backgrounds discuss the topic of the moment with great vigor, whether or not they know anything about it. Music is popular as well. If you see a violin or wind instrument hanging on the wall, feel free to take it down and play it.

Don't be surprised if you find yourself sharing more than conversation with your fellow travelers. At dinner, you will probably share a trencher (a hollowed out block of wood like a large soup bowl) with another person. A single drinking glass, usually made from leather or wood and sometimes holding as much as one gallon, is passed up and down the table for all to share.

If you wish to stay the night, you can rent bed space. Each room holds several beds, all of them probably already occupied by strangers. You could find yourself in a bed with as many as five other people. Every

*The Indian Queen Tavern in Bladensburg, Maryland, rents rooms to tired travelers.*

## Hot Hint

The rule of the road is "no boots, no spurs" in bed.

other person lies with his or her head at the head of the bed. The others lie with their heads at the foot of the bed, so you will be up close and personal with your fellow travelers' feet, not their faces.

By the way, if you feel something squirming in the bed, you've found a bedbug, a common colonial companion. Roaches are also frequent roommates. Inns vary in quality and cleanliness.

You won't find many women in public inns. The few women who travel generally arrange to stay in private homes with people they know (colonists don't consider it proper for a woman to travel alone). Some inns have single rooms, and women occasionally use them when they travel.

Inns are plentiful and inexpensive in the northern colonies. In Salem, for example, you can get lodging, food, and beverages for just three shillings. Inns are harder to find in Virginia or the Carolinas, but you will find it easy to stay in private homes there.

# What to Eat

*This undated illustration depicts Pilgrims and Native Americans sharing food.*

## Mealtime

Housewives and cooks begin preparing meals as early as four o'clock in the morning by hauling water and building up the fire. After the other members of the family have been at work for a couple of hours, the women serve a large breakfast. The main meal of the day is ready by two o'clock in the afternoon. In the evening, you may get another run at the main meal in the form of cold leftovers.

On baking days, meals are generally lighter, since the cooks are busy. On Fridays, many people eat fish. This is a religious custom for some people. It also helps promote the sale of fish.

# Common Foods

Food tends to be simple and in good supply. You will see a lot of corn—and not just as food. The cobs are used as stoppers for jugs, handles for tools, and bowls for pipes. People also eat turkey, chicken, beef, mutton, and tripe (stomach tissue). Deer are common, so venison is easy to get. In the Chesapeake region, you may dine on ducks, geese, and other waterfowl.

Pork tends to be the most common meat. Pigs are cheap to raise since they can find food on their own in the woods, and they produce a lot of meat. Colonists use every part of a pig to produce many valuable items. A pig's bladder, for example, can be used as a container.

Hosts often show their generosity by the amount and variety of meat they serve. A visitor to New York reported that at one meal he was served a haunch of venison that weighed 30 pounds, wild turkey, and wild goose. Later, his host persuaded him to taste some raccoon. "It was very fat and of a good flavor," the visitor thought, "almost like a pig."

Seafood is plentiful along the coast. Colonists harvest so many oysters in the harbors of New York that they feed them to hogs by the bushel. The streams are full of fish.

## Foods to Try

- Apple butter—peeled apples boiled down with cider to a butterlike consistency
- Suckets—dried sweets, such as candied orange peel
- Dried fruit—berries or other fruit, mashed into a paste and then dried, similar to modern fruit roll-ups

# TAKE IT from a Local

Stuff not thy mouth so as to fill thy Cheeks;
be content with smaller Mouthfuls.
—*from* The School of Manners, *1701*

If you travel in winter, you'll find that fresh fruits and vegetables are not available to ordinary people. Spices and perfumes help disguise the lack of freshness in foods. Many foods are dried. You may see strings of peppers, apples, or pumpkins hanging from poles near the fireplace to dry.

Colonists eat preserved food all year, since they have no refrigeration. They pickle cabbage, flower buds, green walnuts, lemons, parsley, mushrooms, asparagus, and fruit. They smoke meat and salt fish, leaving it to dry on racks in the sun. The smell of the fish and the sight of flies landing on it may not do much for your appetite.

Wealthy people eat more lavishly than common folk. They can buy luxury items such as imported almonds, spices, pepper, raisins, and salt from all over the world. The wealthy are particularly fond of desserts. You may see such treats as "lemon creame," "orange biskett," and "cheese cakes of oranges."

Don't overindulge in the local delicacies. Some colonists believe newcomers tend to make themselves sick by their "own folly or excesses" in enjoying colonial foods. Colonists call this tendency "seasoning."

Many native people in the northern colonies grow corn. They use almost every part of the corn plant. They braid the husks to make moccasins, baskets, and cornhusk dolls. They burn corncobs as fuel.

Native people eat corn at almost every meal. Corn is eaten fresh or cooked, or used in corn soup, corn syrup, succotash (corn mixed with beans), and other foods.

*Native Americans show early colonists how to grow corn and gather many North American foods.*

Corn can be dried and then eaten throughout the cold months of the year. Hominy is dried corn that has been soaked in a mixture of water and ashes, then rinsed and stir fried.

Cornmeal is made by grinding corn. It is used to prepare cornbread, corn pudding, and other foods. Native people also boil cornmeal together with maple syrup to make a special dessert.

The colonists had never eaten corn before native people shared corn with them. Corn saves the lives of many early colonists.

Handy
WORDS & PHRASES

Succotash is a Native American dish made from corn and lima beans.

69

# FOODS TO TRY,
*at your own risk*

- Pemmican—shredded, dried meat in fat, combined with wild cherries or other dried fruit and sugar. Popular with explorers, frontiersmen, and travelers.

- Fried beaver tail—speaks for itself

- Hardtack—a bread made from flour and water that has been dried to such a hardness that it can last fifty years. Although hardtack is often infested with weevils (insects), their burrows actually make this bread easier to chew. One of the few foods available on long ship voyages.

# DINING ON A BUDGET

The lower classes eat bland and unvaried food. The most common dishes are soups and stews (vegetables—with or without meat—boiled together in huge pots on the fire). Most colonists won't try foods that are native to America (such as sweet potatoes) but not known in Europe.

Colonists do adapt some recipes for European dishes to the ingredients available in America. If you stay with a Dutch or German family, you may get sauerkraut, coleslaw, cookies, and crullers (a sort of donut). The French make good fish chowders. The English favor apple pie and stews with root vegetables such as parsnips, turnips, and carrots.

In season, you will get wonderful berries—huckleberries, blackberries, blueberries, and wild strawberries. Although the colonists marvel at the "natural" abundance of berries, it is actually the result of Native American land management. The Indians use controlled burning of undergrowth to increase the growth of berry vines.

Most farms have an orchard, usually with apple or peach trees. You'll probably eat apple pie at least once, particularly if you are traveling through New England. Cooks prepare this favorite dish year-round, using dried apples when fresh ones are not available. Children often get apple pie as their evening meal.

When dinner is served, people sit "at the board." The table in an ordinary home is literally a board set on trestles (a braced frame serving as a support) and covered by a cloth, if the family has one. This is where the expression "room and board" comes from. You will sit on a chest, bench, or stool pulled up to the board—chairs are a luxury. If the family has a chair, it is reserved for the man of the house. The expression "chairman" began this way.

Sweets are easy to find. Almost every good-sized town has a bakery where you can buy cookies, cakes, and other treats. Colonists make maple sugar by tapping sugar maple trees and boiling down the sap. They also use honey for sweetening. People can buy sugar loaves (huge blocks or cones of sugar weighing nine or ten pounds each). Ginger, almonds, rock candy, and raisins come in by boat from Europe.

# Do You Want a Beverage with That?

Don't visit before 1712 if you want tea (perhaps anticipating a certain tea party in Boston). There isn't any. Tea, which is grown in India, isn't available in England until the mid-1600s and doesn't arrive in the colonies until after 1712. Coffee does not arrive in the area until the early 1800s. Apple cider is popular. People usually make it from their own apple trees.

The colonists are not used to drinking water (Europeans drink beer, ale, or wine). They drink water only when necessary, since they aren't sure whether local water causes diseases or not.

If you like milk, visit during the 1700s, when cows are plentiful and milk becomes a part of everyday meals. People often eat bread and milk for breakfast and sometimes even for supper.

# WHERE TO FIND SOUVENIRS

## ARTS, CRAFTS, & OTHER DELIGHTS

Quilts come in an amazing array of colors and patterns with fanciful names such as "Dove in the Window," "Crow's Foot," and "Sugar-bowl." To make a quilt, women first piece together the quilt top from scraps of fabric. Then they lay down a sheet of plain cloth, cover it with wool or cotton wadding, place the pieced fabric sheet on top, and sew the layers together. Sometimes women do this work together at a quilting bee.

Colonial women make quilts from any bits of cloth available. They may use chintz or calico fabric made from cotton grown in India and manufactured in France. They may use worn-out woolen clothing, old militia uniforms, discarded sheets, or even old underwear. George Washington has a quilt made from silk and pieces of a wedding gown.

Silver crafts are among the best souvenirs of your trip to colonial America. John Hull of Boston is one of the many wonderful goldsmiths and silversmiths in the colonies. His works are expensive, but they are of the highest quality. You will have to travel later to meet the most famous silversmith, Paul Revere, who isn't born until 1735.

*During a quilting bee, women gossip as they work together on a quilt.*

72

# BEST BUYS

Clothing made from fur and animal hides is popular in the northern colonies as well as in Europe. You may find gloves, jackets, and other clothing made from deerskin. These garments are buttery soft and long wearing.

Native Americans and colonists both trap beaver, mink, and other fur-bearing animals. You can buy fur coats and hats made of beaver felt (beaver skin treated to make it flat and smooth). Other best buys include bayberry candles or weather vanes in the shapes of roosters, fish, horses, or even lions.

*A weather vane*

# How to Stay Safe & Healthy

*Following the saying "Love is the best physician," family and friends gather at the bedside of a sick man.*

## Take Some Devil's Dung and Call Me in the Morning

You'll find many health hazards in the colonies, so be careful. The death rate is particularly high before the 1640s, so you may want to travel after that period. From 1619 to 1623 in Virginia, about 75 percent of the colony's population dies, mostly because of a smallpox epidemic.

*During the 1600s, a large number of Wampanoag people die of diseases introduced by the European settlers.*

Smallpox epidemics occur about every ten or fifteen years. The symptoms are horrifying—severe headache, fever, convulsions, delirium, and a blistering rash. These afflictions quickly weaken the body, often causing death.

Smallpox also devastates Native Americans. From 1617 to 1619, smallpox kills 90 percent of the native people of the Massachusetts Bay area. Another outbreak, in Connecticut in 1634, kills 95 percent of the Native Americans living along the Connecticut River.

The colonists have found no "new" diseases here. The diseases you are exposed to will be those the settlers brought with them from Europe or the West Indies—whooping cough, influenza, and tuberculosis in addition to smallpox.

Typhoid and dysentery are common diseases in the Chesapeake region. So is malaria, since it is spread by the mosquitoes that breed in the region's many swamps. Although malaria won't kill you, it can leave you so weak that another disease will. In New England, the climate is healthier, and residents live longer than the people in the southern colonies. In Andover, Massachusetts, for example, three men in ten (and almost as many women) live to the age of seventy.

Yellow fever is another deadly disease. Colonists think it spreads from person to person. But actually it is transmitted by mosquitoes. Symptoms include yellowish skin and black vomit. In the summer, stay away from areas near standing water, where mosquitoes breed.

Female family members, not physicians, do most of the everyday doctoring in colonial America. Professional doctors charge a lot. In 1655, for example, a carpenter earns six hundred pounds of tobacco for building a house. A doctor gets one thousand pounds or more for attending patients. After 1736 many colonists rely on a book called *Every Man His Own Doctor*, which was published that year. It describes symptoms and cures for common diseases.

Medical treatments aren't very pleasant. If you get a fever, the doctor will want to drain your body of "morbific matter." The first step is for the doctor to cut you so that you lose some blood. After that the doctor will probably give you a purge, which forces you to empty your bowels (get a head start to the outdoor privy!). Once you're cleaned out, you take some medicine.

If you think medicine tastes and smells bad at home, you are in for a shock. In colonial America, medicines are meant to smell foul. The stink supposedly revives the patient. One smelly common herb is called "devil's dung" because it smells like, well, devil's dung.

*Physicians practice bloodletting to help cure many ailments.*

Native Americans use plants to make medicines that are often more effective than the ones a colonial doctor may give you. For example, some Native American groups treat scurvy with a tea made from black spruce needles, which are rich in vitamin C. This makes sense, since scurvy is a disease caused by lack of vitamin C. The colonists think scurvy is caused by breathing bad air or eating too much salted meat.

**IMPORTANT**
*Safety Tip*

Drink cider rather than water; it's safer, particularly in the Chesapeake region. Wells contaminated with sewage contribute to the high rates of the deadly diseases typhoid and dysentery.

Colonial doctors have no anesthetics and no way to replace lost blood, so operations tend to be fast. Real fast. Most last only a couple of minutes. To help fight the pain, doctors give the patient something to bite down on. Then family members or friends hold the patient down (often on the kitchen table) as the doctor operates. With any luck, the patient passes out. The greatest danger comes later, from infection, as the patient recovers.

## WATCH FOR WARS

In some areas, settlers and Native Americans live peacefully as neighbors. In fact, native people often act as guides, trackers, and interpreters for colonists. They also provide valuable advice on growing crops.

Disputes over land and other disagreements, however, lead to full-scale battles. In the Connecticut River Valley, a smallpox epidemic between 1634 and 1635 kills the people in one Indian settlement. Another native group, the Pequots, take over the territory, much to the displeasure of the nearby Narragansetts. Meanwhile, the people of the Massachusetts Bay Colony also want the land.

When two white traders are mysteriously killed in Pequot territory, the colonists, with the help of the Narragansetts, go after the Pequots.

*Disputes over land and other disagreements between the Pequots and the colonists lead to war.*

The Pequots strike back in 1637, surprising nearby settlers and killing nine people. The colonists take revenge by burning alive about five hundred Indian people, mostly women and children. They then surround the Pequot warriors, killing many and selling the rest into slavery.

# LAW & ORDER

Even with lots of lonely woods and trails, thievery is uncommon in most areas. In New England cities, watchmen walk the streets at night, checking to be sure the lanterns are lit, watching for fires and thieves, and calling out the time and the weather. New York has ten watchmen by 1658. They rattle a "klopper" (bell) as they patrol to keep any thieves away. You may also hear them calling "One o'clock and all's well" or "Two o'clock and fair winds."

Colonial America has jails, but they are mainly for people who owe money or who have nowhere else to go. Whippings are a more common punishment than a jail sentence. The criminal (male or female) is whipped on the bare back. The whip, or "cat-o'-nine tails," has a number

*Puritans are known to punish lawbreakers with public whippings.*

of leather tails, each knotted at the end. At each stroke of this whip, the tails bite into the bare flesh. Twenty lashes to more than one hundred lashes may be given. Sentences of more than forty lashes can be fatal. The flesh on the back eventually falls away, causing extensive bleeding and exposing internal organs.

You may notice that punishments don't always seem fair. The common folk are routinely sentenced to public whippings. Wealthy gentlemen, however, are usually excused from such humiliations. An ordinary citizen must sit on the sharp edge of a board while in the stocks. A gentleman may stand.

You may have heard of the stocks (boards with holes to hold the criminal's ankles) or the pillory (boards with holes for the head and hands). Being locked into one of these restraining devices for a while may seem like a mild physical discomfort. The real discomfort is humiliation, since prisoners are set in a public place, and people throw eggs, rotten fruit, or tomatoes at them.

Another punishment is to be "burned at the hand." The name of the crime is burned into the criminal's skin just below the thumb on the right hand as a permanent record of wrongdoing.

*Another form of
punishment by the
colonists is to be
locked in the stocks
or in the pillory.*

*A Puritan father punishes his son by catching him by the ear and leading him home while villagers look on.*

Be sure to watch your manners. You can be fined and punished for such criminal acts as calling people names, making nasty faces, lying, or jeering. One Virginia man made "base and detracting" remarks about the governor. As punishment, his arms were broken and his tongue was punctured with an awl before he was fined and banished.

# WEATHER DISASTERS
# & OTHER ANNOYANCES

Some aspects of the climate are a complete surprise to colonists. Severe storms, especially hurricanes, astonish the settlers, who saw no such weather in Europe. During the colonial period, many hurricanes and other severe storms strike the colonies. A hurricane that hits Virginia in 1667 destroys ten thousand houses and almost all the crops.

Harsh weather leads to crop failures in early colonial times. The settlers struggle to grow crops in an unfamiliar climate. Often they fail. To make matters worse, repeated droughts—prolonged periods of dryness—devastate crops.

Droughts trigger starving times, when settlements have no food. On Roanoke Island, North Carolina, a drought from 1587 to 1589 contributes to many deaths. All trace of the colony disappears by the time ships from England return with supplies. Another extreme drought hits Jamestown, Virginia, from 1606 to 1612. Over half the residents perish, many from hunger.

Also in Jamestown, the first settlers fail to plant crops that can survive in the New World, thus remaining dependent on the Powhatans. When the drought reduces food supplies, the settlers demand food from the Powhatans. The once-friendly Powhatans deny their requests in an attempt to drive the settlers away.

# WHO'S WHO IN COLONIAL AMERICA

## BENJAMIN FRANKLIN

If you happen to be in Philadelphia in 1723, look up Benjamin Franklin. He recently arrived from Boston (with only one Dutch guilder and one English shilling in his pocket). He is working for a printer named Samuel Keimer. You may have trouble recognizing him if you have only seen pictures of him as a white-haired patriot. In 1723 he is seventeen years old.

If you travel later, you will find Franklin has his own printing business. From 1732 to 1757, you will be able to pick up copies of his *Poor Richard's Almanac*, a great source of advice and tips for success in business, such as, "Early to bed and early to rise, Makes a man healthy, wealthy, and wise."

## COTTON MATHER

As a boy, Cotton Mather was teased for spending all his time studying, praying, reading, and writing sermons. All his studying paid off, though. He entered Harvard University at age eleven and began preaching at seventeen. As an adult, he reads and speaks seven languages and has written over four hundred books.

Although he is not known as a fun-loving person, Mather considers himself "a man whose Business it is to do good unto all." He operates a school for African American students in Boston and also helps widows, orphans, prisoners, Native Americans, and the poor. He is so generous that by 1721, he owns no land, having spent everything on charity.

## WILLIAM PENN

King Charles II of England owed William Penn a debt originally owed to Penn's father. In 1680 Penn asked the king for a bit of land in repayment and received—get this—*Pennsylvania*. Actually, Penn proposed "Sylvania" as the colony's name. He even offered twenty guineas to have his name removed because he thought it vain. The secretary of the colony added "Penn" despite Penn's protests.

Penn is a Quaker who at one time had been jailed in the Tower of London for his religious beliefs. He sees his new colony as a "Holy Experiment" where Quakers can worship as they please. Penn may be difficult to meet because he frequently returns to England to settle business and political matters.

Penn is known for his ability to negotiate treaties with Native Americans. His Charter of Liberties and Privileges of 1701 establishes a form of government that allows the people of his colony to govern themselves. It also prevents anyone—even himself—from having too much power.

## POCAHONTAS

You might like to meet the real Pocahontas while visiting Jamestown. She is Powhatan's daughter. She was twelve years old when she met John Smith—a little younger than she looks in the Walt Disney movie *Pocahontas*.

Jamestown colonist John Smith later wrote that Pocahontas saved his life. He said he had been captured by Powhatan. Pocahontas threw herself in front of John Smith to stop Powhatan from beating him with a club. Pocahontas eventually marries John Rolfe of

Jamestown. They have a child named Thomas Rolfe. Some modern Americans can trace their ancestry back to Thomas Rolfe, John Rolfe, and Pocahontas.

# Edward Teach (Blackbeard)

The fiercest of all the pirates, a man named Edward Teach has earned the nickname "Blackbeard." He is known as a "swaggering, merciless brute." If anything, that's being kind. He is certainly an interesting character if you have a chance to meet him someplace other than on the receiving end of a pirate raid. Tall and muscular, with a long, bushy, ink-black beard, this man wears a strap across his chest to hold six pistols, all cocked and ready to fire. In his belt are daggers, more pistols, and a large sword. Braided pigtails stick out from his hair and beard, and before battle, he sticks long, slow-burning matches under his hat. This awesome sight leads some ship passengers to think that the Devil himself is coming aboard.

Blackbeard commands a cannon-packed ship called *Queen Anne's Revenge*. He uses it to attack ships traveling the trade route between the colonies and the West Indies (a region of islands in the Caribbean Sea). He even picks off vessels just outside the busy port city of Charleston. Look for him from about 1714 to 1718 around the Ocracoke Inlet of North Carolina, where he has several hideouts. He is caught and executed in 1718, ending an era of piracy.

# Weetamoo

Weetamoo is a Wampanoag woman who married the eldest son of Massasoit, the Indian leader who befriended the Pilgrims at Plymouth in 1620. When Weetamoo's husband dies, she becomes the leader of a large village, Pocasset.

With more than three hundred warriors at her command, Weetamoo controls land that several colonies would like to have. She wants to continue the peace with the settlers. At the same time, however, she objects to her people's loss of land and authority. By 1675 she gives up on peaceful negotiation and leads her soldiers into battle.

A year later, Weetamoo and the people with her are ambushed by the Puritans in the area. According to Increase Mather, a Puritan minister, Weetamoo survives the attack. Later, however, he reports seeing her head on a pole.

# PREPARING FOR THE TRIP

## PLAY NINE MEN'S MORRIS

Playing Nine Men's Morris is a bit like playing Ultimate Tic Tac Toe. You will need:

> two players
> playing board
> nine playing pieces for each player

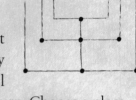

To make a playing board, copy the diagram at right on a piece of paper. For playing pieces, choose any small object a colonist might have, such as small stones. To play, put one piece on the board on each turn. Choose a place where the lines meet. Your opponent then does the same. If you get three pieces in a row, take one of your opponent's pieces off the board.

After all your pieces are in play, you can begin moving them around on the board. Move pieces by sliding them to a neighboring unoccupied intersection. Continue trying to get three pieces in a row so that you can capture your opponent's pieces.

Eventually one player will have just three pieces left. That player can then move pieces to any unoccupied intersection on the board. When one player has just two pieces left, he or she loses. The game is over.

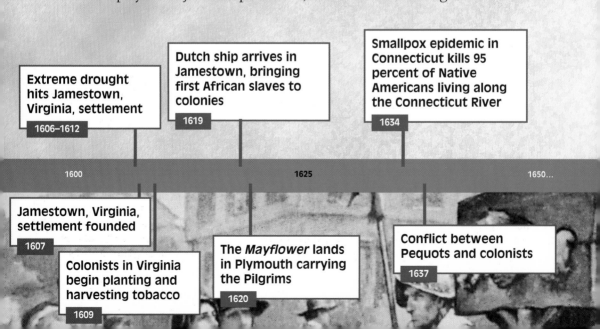

**Extreme drought hits Jamestown, Virginia, settlement**
1606–1612

**Dutch ship arrives in Jamestown, bringing first African slaves to colonies**
1619

**Smallpox epidemic in Connecticut kills 95 percent of Native Americans living along the Connecticut River**
1634

**Jamestown, Virginia, settlement founded**
1607

**Colonists in Virginia begin planting and harvesting tobacco**
1609

**The *Mayflower* lands in Plymouth carrying the Pilgrims**
1620

**Conflict between Pequots and colonists**
1637

1600    1625    1650...

# MAKE A SIGN

Have you ever wanted to run your own business? Try making a sign for a business you might own in colonial America. You will need:

> scratch paper
> pencil
> white poster paper
> colored markers, crayons, or poster paint

Your sign tells customers what you sell, make, or repair. But many colonists can't read. So be sure to include a picture. A simple drawing of an object works well.

What kind of object might advertise the shop of a blacksmith, brickmaker, dressmaker, hatmaker, printer, tavern keeper, or wigmaker? Think about an object that would explain what you sell, make, or repair.

Next, make a rough copy of your sign. Sketch your object. Then sketch a border around it. People need to see your sign clearly from a distance, so keep everything simple and big.

Then reach for the poster paper and colored markers, crayons, or paints. Be bold with color. As a last step, cut around the outside edge of your border.

If your whole class joins in, you can hang up all the signs. Your classroom will look like main street in a colonial village!

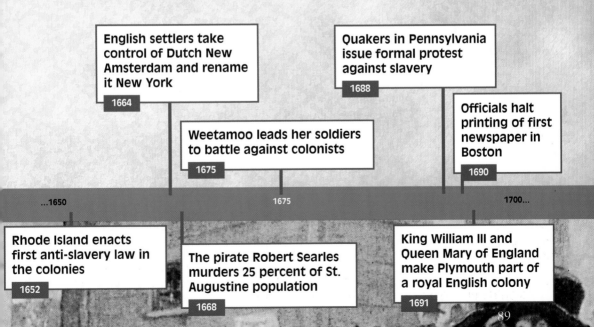

**English settlers take control of Dutch New Amsterdam and rename it New York**
1664

**Quakers in Pennsylvania issue formal protest against slavery**
1688

**Officials halt printing of first newspaper in Boston**
1690

**Weetamoo leads her soldiers to battle against colonists**
1675

...1650          1675          1700...

**Rhode Island enacts first anti-slavery law in the colonies**
1652

**The pirate Robert Searles murders 25 percent of St. Augustine population**
1668

**King William III and Queen Mary of England make Plymouth part of a royal English colony**
1691

89

# GLOSSARY

**bee:** a gathering of people for a specific purpose, usually to complete a task of some kind. Two examples are chopping bees and quilting bees.

**bulrush:** a large, grasslike marsh plant that can be woven into mats and chair seats

**Church of England:** the Protestant church created in England in 1534 after King Henry VIII decided to leave the Roman Catholic Church

**muster:** a formal inspection or drill of a military unit

**Pilgrim:** a person who travels to foreign lands, especially for religious reasons. When this word is capitalized, it refers specifically to one group of colonists who came to Plymouth on the *Mayflower* in 1620.

**Protestant:** a member of a Christian—but not Catholic—church. A few of the many Protestant denominations are the Anglicans, Lutherans, and Puritans.

**Puritan:** a member of a Protestant group in England and New England in the 1500s and 1600s who followed a strict moral code

**Quaker:** a member of the Religious Society of Friends, a religious group. Most Quakers in colonial America settled in Rhode Island and Pennsylvania.

**smallpox:** a very contagious disease that causes the victim to run a high fever and to break out in severe blisters. Vaccination and control measures in modern times have nearly eliminated smallpox worldwide.

**wigwam:** a hutlike dwelling used by many Native Americans living east of the Mississippi River in the 1600s

**witchcraft:** the use of sorcery or magic. Many colonial Americans believed in witchcraft. Witches—people who practiced witchcraft—were usually thought to be in communication with the Devil.

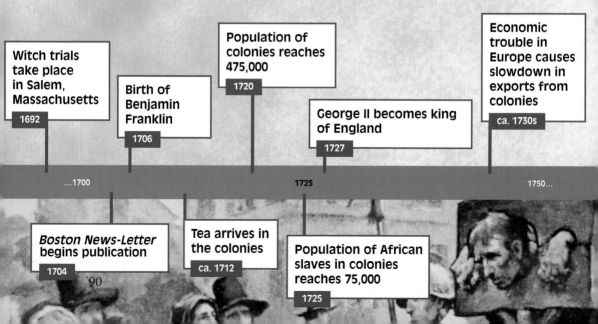

Witch trials take place in Salem, Massachusetts
1692

Birth of Benjamin Franklin
1706

Population of colonies reaches 475,000
1720

George II becomes king of England
1727

Economic trouble in Europe causes slowdown in exports from colonies
ca. 1730s

...1700

1725

1750...

*Boston News-Letter* begins publication
1704

Tea arrives in the colonies
ca. 1712

Population of African slaves in colonies reaches 75,000
1725

90

# PRONUNCIATION GUIDE

| | |
|---|---|
| **Anglican** | AYNG-glih-kuhn |
| **Cotton Mather** | KAH-tuhn MA-thur |
| **etiquette** | EH-tih-kuht |
| **Hopi** | HOH-pee |
| **Massasoit** | mas-uh-SOYT |
| **Narragansett** | nehr-uh-GAN-suht |
| **pemmican** | PEH-mih-kuhn |
| **Pequot** | PEE-kwaht |
| **Powhatan** | pow-uh-TAN |
| **Puritan** | PYOOR-ih-tuhn |
| **Samoset** | SAM-uh-seht |
| **Squanto** | SKWAHN-toh |
| **succotash** | SUH-kuh-tash |
| **Wampanoag** | wahm-puh-NOH-ag |

**American Revolution begins**

1776

*Poor Richard's Almanac* in publication

1732–1757

...1750

1775

1800

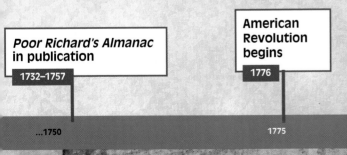

# FURTHER READING

Barrett, Tracey. *Growing Up in Colonial America*. Brookfield, CT: The Millbrook Press, 1995.

Greene, Meg. *Slave Young, Slave Long: The American Slave Experience*. Minneapolis: Lerner Publications Company, 1999.

Hakim, Joy. *The First Americans*. New York: Oxford University Press, 1999.

Knight, James E., et al. *The Village: Life in Colonial Times*. Mahwah, NJ: Troll Associates, 1998.

Ofosu-Appiah, L. H. *People in Bondage: African Slavery Since the 15th Century*. Minneapolis: Runestone Press, 1993.

Wilson, Lori Lee. *The Salem Witch Trials*. Minneapolis: Lerner Publications Company, 1997.

Wood, Peter H. *Strange New Land: African Americans, 1617–1776*. New York: Oxford University Press, 1996.

Young, Robert. *A Personal Tour of Monticello*. Minneapolis: Lerner Publications Company, 1999.

# INTERNET SITES

*A Colonial Family and Community*
<http://www.hfmgv.org/smartfun/colonial/intro/index.html>

*Colonial Williamsburg's Historical Almanack*
<http://www.history.org/almanack.htm>

*Virtual Jamestown*
<http://jefferson.village.virginia.edu/vcdh/jamestown>

# BIBLIOGRAPHY

Adams, James Truslow. "Provincial Society, 1690–1763." In *A History of American Life,* edited by Arthur M. Schlesinger Sr. and Dixon Ryan Fox. New York: Scribner, 1996.

Berkin, Carol. *First Generations: Women in Colonial America.* New York: Hill and Wang, 1996.

Dill, Jordan S. "Wampanoag History," *First Nations Site.* n.d. <http://www.dickshovel.com/wampa.html> (November 2, 1999).

Glubok, Shirley, ed. *Home and Child Life in Colonial Days.* New York: The Macmillan Company, 1969.

Hawke, David Freeman. *Everyday Life in Early America.* New York: Harper & Row, 1989.

McKay, John P., Bennett D. Hill, and John Buckler. A *History of World Societies.* Vol II. Boston: Houghton Mifflin Company, 1992.

Miller, John C. *The Colonial Image: Origins of American Culture.* New York: George Braziller, 1962.

Morris, Richard B., ed. *The Beginnings of America 1607–1763.* St. Louis, MO: Webster Division, McGraw-Hill Book Company, 1961.

Plimoth Plantation. *Plimoth-on-Web.* n.d. <http://www.plimoth.org> (November 2, 1999).

Reader's Digest. *Everyday Life Through the Ages.* London: The Reader's Digest Association, 1992.

Robert E. Lee Memorial Association. "Education for Boys and Girls." *Stratford Hall Site.* n.d. <http://www.stratfordhall.org/ed-boysgirls.htm> (April 2, 1998).

Robert E. Lee Memorial Association. "Leisure Time and Games." *Stratford Hall Site.* n.d. <http://www.stratfordhall.org/ed-games.htm> (April 2, 1998).

Tannahill, Reay. *Food in History.* New York: Stein and Day Publishers, 1973.

Taylor, Dale. *The Writer's Guide to Everyday Life in Colonial America.* Cincinnati, OH: Writer's Digest Books, 1997.

Wolf, Stephanie Grauman. *As Various as Their Land: The Everyday Lives of Eighteenth-Century Americans.* New York: HarperCollins, 1994.

Wright, Louis B. *Everyday Life in Colonial America.* New York: G. P. Putnam's Sons, 1965.

# INDEX

# ABOUT THE AUTHOR

Nancy Day is the author of nine books and forty-five articles for young people. She loves to read and is fascinated with the idea of time travel, which she says is "actually history in a great disguise." Her interest in time travel inspired the Passport to History series. Nancy Day lives with her husband, son, and two cats in a house that was built in 1827 before the Civil War. She often imagines what it would be like to go back in time to meet the shipbuilder who once lived there.

**Acknowledgments for Quoted Material** pp. 37, 43, as quoted by David Freeman Hawke, *Everyday Life in Early America* (New York: Harper & Row, 1989); p. 56, as quoted by Robert Beverley, "Virginia." *The Colonial Image: Origins of American Culture*, John C. Miller, ed. (New York: George Braziller, 1962); p. 68, as quoted by Shirley Glubok, ed., *Home and Child Life in Colonial Days* (New York: The Macmillan Company, 1969).

**Photo Acknowledgments**
© Library of Congress/The Bridgeman Art Library, London/New York, p. 2; © Mary Evans Picture Library, pp. 6–7, 85 (top), 86; © Archive Photos, pp. 11, 36, 54, 60, 79, 84 (both), 85 (bottom); © North Wind Picture Archives, pp. 12, 14–15, 16, 22, 24, 25, 26, 30–31, 33, 39, 42, 49, 58–59, 69, 76; © Culver Pictures, pp. 19, 61, 63, 72–73, 75, 77; © CORBIS/Bettmann, pp. 20, 34, 35, 44, 45, 51, 55, 56, 74, 80–81, 81 (bottom), 82, 88–89, 90–91; © The Granger Collection, New York, pp. 27, 67; © Stock Montage, Inc., pp. 28, 57; © Library of Congress, p. 40; © The Newark Museum/Art Resource, NY, pp. 46, 62; © CORBIS, p. 64; © American Stock/Archive Photos, p. 66.

Front cover: © Science Museum, London, UK/The Bridgeman Art Library, London/New York (top); © Private Collection/The Bridgeman Art Library, London/New York (bottom).